PRAISE FOR
101 PRESIDENTIAL INSULTS:
What They Really Thought About Each Other –
and What It Means to Us

"Mike Purdy has written a terrific book. As a presidential historian, he has a gift for discovering just the right anecdotes that help us understand our presidents better. Really well done."

– PAUL BRANDUS
White House bureau chief, West Wing Reports,
USA Today columnist,
Author of *Under This Roof: The White House and Presidency*

"Filthy, disgraced, lying, cheating, calculating bastard, schemer, a dangerous man, a little schmuck, unfit to serve...Mike Purdy brings us into the political locker room, where nothing is left unsaid. This book is a statement on the dark humanity of American presidents— sad and hilarious, at the same time."

– A.J. BAIME
New York Times bestselling author of *The Accidental President*
and *The Arsenal of Democracy*

"Mike Purdy provides a picture of these presidents as flawed or, rather, human leaders—prone to the pettiness, anger, and incivility that even the best of us exhibit. This book should be required reading for those concerned about the current political climate. Perhaps in knowing the past we can chart a new, more civil course. It's also great reading for those who enjoy a good laugh!"

– DR. MICHAEL ARTIME
Visiting Assistant Professor of Political Science at
Pacific Lutheran University (Tacoma, Washington)

"In *101 Presidential Insults*, Mike Purdy shows us that the art of the presidential insult is not a new phenomenon, but in fact has been part of American history since the founding. What has changed, however, is the platform: from private letters, to a national audience, and finally to insults amplified instantly around the globe across social media. Purdy has meticulously selected some of the most rancorous and ridiculous presidential barbs that are sure to both entertain and inform. Because while history may not repeat itself, Purdy show us that it does seem pretty darned familiar sometimes."

– LOUIS L. PICONE
Author of *Where the Presidents Were Born*
and *The President is Dead!*

"Mike Purdy, a prolific Presidential historian, has come up with a new angle about the Presidency, Presidential insults by Presidents against other Presidents. It is a unique and fascinating look at the 44 men who have served as President and makes them look more human. The constant insults of Donald Trump might seem to be new in the intensity and frequency of his attacks on other Presidents, but this book demonstrates that other Presidents, before the age of Twitter and mass audiences and round the clock news media, were quite competitive in their insults of other Presidents historically, contemporaneously, and in retrospect. Anyone reading this book will have reactions of laughter, shock, and amazement as they learn more about the personalities of our 44 Presidents. This book is highly recommended to all who follow and love the institution of the American Presidency."

– DR. RONALD L. FEINMAN
Author of *Assassinations, Threats, and the American Presidency*

"Mike Purdy's track on *101 Presidential Insults* reveals a side of presidential politics that is at once delightful and shocking. We will see plenty of mudslinging going into the 2020 election, but *101 Presidential Insults* reminds us that it really has always been that way."

– THE HONORABLE DON BONKER
Former Member of Congress

"Mike Purdy's book is an addictive and refreshing read for any lover of American history. A delightful concept – executed masterfully – it explores some of the most un-presidential moments of the American presidency. The book is a helpful reminder in frustrating times that combative political mudslinging is not something new, and always painfully funny. Put simply, Mike Purdy is one hell of a historian."

– ROBERT BUCCELLATO
Author of *Jimmy Carter in Plains: The Presidential Hometown*

"Who knew that there was so much jealousy, backbiting, petty put-downs and outright slander directed at each other among our illustrious U.S. presidents? Mike Purdy's prodigious research has dug out the juicy bits that are often declared out-of-bounds in presidential biographies. He's managed to assemble more venom than you thought possible in the Oval Office. What's more, in this delightful and breezy volume, there are laughs and insights aplenty. Mike Purdy has shown us through these well-selected quotations a side of our presidents we had never known, or perhaps purposely kept under wraps. After reading this book, you'll never look at the commander-in-chief the same way again."

– PAUL GRONDAHL
Author of *I Rose Like a Rocket:*
The Political Education of Theodore Roosevelt

"Mike Purdy's book, albeit brief, is quite a read. I assumed that today's politics was slam bang with its polarization, big money hit pieces and slanted news coverage. But the barbs and name calling we see now is small stuff compared to the good old days. Let's see: Abe Lincoln was a person of "narrow intelligence" and Franklin Roosevelt was a "gibbering idiot". And these were some of the great presidents. The book is an eye opener."

– DR. BILL BAARSMA
Former Mayor
City of Tacoma, Washington

"What a nifty and enjoyable little tome of caustic, colorful, insightful and frequently witty comments by our Presidents - about each other! They were indeed human, with all the sparkle and foibles of real people!"

– FEATHER SCHWARTZ FOSTER
Author of *The First Ladies,* and
*Mary Lincoln's Flannel Pajamas
and Other Stories from the First Ladies' Closet*

101

PRESIDENTIAL INSULTS

What They Really Thought
About Each Other –
and What It Means to Us

101
PRESIDENTIAL INSULTS

What They Really Thought
About Each Other –
and What It Means to Us

Mike Purdy

PRESIDENTIAL HISTORY PRESS
Seattle • 2019

Refer all questions or inquiries to:
Mike Purdy
PO Box 46181
Seattle, WA 98146-0181
or by email to Mike@PresidentialHistory.com

www.PresidentialHistory.com

ISBN 978-1-54396-374-8 (print)

ISBN 978-1-54396-375-5 (ebook)

Cover illustration: Copyright © 2019 by Victor Juhasz

Cover starting at the top center: Donald Trump.
Going clockwise: Harry Truman, John Kennedy,
Richard Nixon, and Theodore Roosevelt.

TABLE OF CONTENTS

AUTHOR'S NOTE

I've always been fascinated by the relationships between the very human and flawed men who have held the office of the presidency. I love patterns and identifying common historical themes. Many years ago, from my presidential history research, I began noticing that our presidents would often snipe about other presidents. I started collecting the quotes and looking for new ones.

This book of 101 negative quotations about the forty-four men who have served as U.S. president – all from the pens and lips of their predecessors and successors – is the result of my research.

I've tried to make this book of insults by the presidents about the presidents more than just a fun collection of quotations. To that end, I've added for each quotation a brief description of the occasion and date. I've cited primary sources when possible, or reputable secondary sources that include footnotes. Some of the quotations have previously appeared in other books but generally without the context and without citing a source. Rather than rely on "unnamed sources," I've researched the quotations to validate each one. I deleted some quotations I originally planned to use because my research and that of others demonstrated there were not solid historical grounds for them.

For example, while Theodore Roosevelt's colorful characterization of William Howard Taft as not having the "brains of a guinea pig" is memorable, I couldn't find a credible reference to it in 1912 when he supposedly said it. If you, the reader, can find such evidence, I would be grateful.

In addition, I deleted William Howard Taft's rebuttal to Theodore Roosevelt that he was a "dangerous demagogue." There are documented sources for him calling Roosevelt a "demagogue" and I've included that in the book, but there is no evidence for "dangerous demagogue." There were other quotes as well that didn't make the final cut.

Before Donald Trump hijacked American politics and became the nation's most prominent and prolific insulter-in-chief, Theodore Roosevelt, Harry Truman, and Richard Nixon were perhaps the most unfiltered (but certainly not only) presidents in trash-talking other members of the exclusive presidential trade union.

Some presidents appear to have flown under the insult radar screen and have been the subject of few attacks by other presidents. Other presidents have served as lightning rods for barbs and insults.

There are clearly more than 101 presidential insults, and the others I've collected will be the subject of a future book or books. I encourage you, the reader, to send me quotes you've discovered. And lest we think the presidents only insulted one another, at times they also spoke highly of one another – maybe another book!

If you, the reader, have any corrections to material in this book I would be grateful if you would let me know.

INTRODUCTION

Donald Trump did not invent the art of the political insult. Sadly, poisonous barbs have been freely and frequently exchanged between our very human presidents since the founding of our republic.

As part of this long and tainted tradition, presidents have let their real feelings about other presidents ooze out in letters, diary entries, conversations, speeches, books, and interviews. Some of the insults are humorous and some are shocking. Often their blunt assessments were made years before the object of their scorn ascended to the presidency. At other times, they vilified a sitting president, a former president, or even dead president.

The interactions between presidents – just like interactions in our families, workplaces, schools, and military – haven't always been civil. Sometimes, their partisan bickering has destroyed once-warm friendships.

It is my hope this unvarnished collection of derisive mudslinging will serve as a call to civility and a means to reset our current political discourse.

Founding Insults

Unfortunately – especially in the age of Trump – we've grown accustomed to politicians delivering biting and slime-coated insults about their colleagues and opponents.

But what's surprising is that the politics of personal destruction is as old as the nation – and the forty-four sometimes distinguished men of the Oval Office have not been immune to dishing out creative and cruel personal attacks on one another. John Adams labeled George Washington as "illiterate." Thomas Jefferson thought Adams was "obstinate." And Jefferson was "ignorant" according to Adams.

What we witness in today's political environment has been around for a long time. The difference today is that Donald Trump's libelous tweets and slanderous barbs are far more unshackled and unfiltered in tone than any of his predecessors. His insults are also significantly more unrelenting in frequency than those of previous presidents. Finally, Trump's insults are more public through his use of social media, while many of our previous presidents voiced their opinions in the privacy of their diaries, letters to trusted friends, or in casual conversations.

Presidential Humanity

All our presidents have been flawed and broken people. They experienced a wide range of emotions – just like all of us. Abraham Lincoln suffered from depression. Thomas Jefferson was terrified of public speaking. William Howard Taft's release from the stress of the presidency was to eat too much. Woodrow Wilson grieved the loss of his wife when he was president. When Calvin Coolidge's teenage son died in the White House, the depressed president lamented that the "power and glory of the presidency went with him."

Our presidents have been filled with – and motivated by – a wide range of human emotions including grief, anger, jealousy, passion, arrogance, envy, and fear. Not surprisingly for men who reached the pinnacle of political power, they were often egotistical and liked being the center of attention. Theodore Roosevelt's daughter, Alice, once famously quipped that her father "always wanted to be the corpse at every funeral, the bride at every wedding, and the baby at every christening."

The presidents often exercised poor judgment in what they wrote and said. Given their humanity, they were often not able to resist the temptation to take their opponents down a notch or two with a sharply worded barb.

Feuds and Friendships

★ ★ ★

The tragedy of some presidential relationships is that one-time friendships often deteriorated into intense verbal vilification of one another, and the men were never reconciled to one another. In other cases, there have been heartwarming reconciliations after seasons of bitterness.

Theodore Roosevelt and William Howard Taft

Theodore Roosevelt and William Howard Taft, once the best of friends and professional colleagues, never fully made up after the bitter 1912 presidential campaign fractured their friendship and split the Republican Party.

When they enjoyed their close partnership, they could joke about their friendship. Roosevelt good-naturedly joshed to Taft after TR's post-presidential African safari that "you have proved to be my best friend, for during my absence the country has turned its attention from my teeth to your stomach," a reference to Roosevelt's wide grin and Taft's wide girth.

A few years later, Roosevelt would denigrate Taft as a "puzzlewit" while Taft warned that his former friend was "to be classed with the leaders of religious cults. I look upon him as I look upon a freak, almost."

While TR and Taft later experienced a cautious and limited reconciliation, their relationship was never the same after they allowed themselves to sink so deeply into the slime of such vicious insults.

Herbert Hoover and Franklin Roosevelt

Another tragic failure in presidential relationships is seen in the enmity that engulfed the partnership of Herbert Hoover and Franklin Roosevelt.

During World War I, Hoover and FDR were good friends, neighbors, and top officials together in the Wilson administration. Roosevelt lobbied for Hoover to run for president, declaring in 1920 that "I wish we could make him President of the United States. There could not be a better one."

A little more than a dozen years later, in the depths of the Depression, the perpetually optimistic Roosevelt ousted the overwhelmed and hapless Hoover from the White House. Hoover angrily berated his successor as "a gibbering idiot" and "a madman."

The relationship between the two on FDR's inauguration day was tense and frosty, and they barely spoke to one another on the awkward ride from the White House to the Capitol. At the conclusion of Roosevelt's inaugural address, Hoover rose, perfunctorily shook the new president's hand, and left immediately for the train that would take him to his political exile in New York City. It was the last time they ever saw one another.

John Adams and Thomas Jefferson

On the other hand, there have been some heart-warming reconciliations between presidents.

Friends and collaborators during the Second Continental Congress that produced the Declaration of Independence and during their diplomatic service together in Europe, John Adams and Thomas Jefferson later became bitter political enemies. They often traded political barbs with one another, with Jefferson maligning Adams as a "poisonous weed," and Adams accusing Jefferson of being "an intriguer."

When Jefferson defeated Adams for the presidency in 1800, an angry, petulant, and disgraced Adams slipped unnoticed out of Washington, D.C. in the early morning hours before Jefferson's inauguration. Adams did not want to witness his successor's moment of triumph.

Nevertheless, in the twilight years of their lives, these two men who had once held great personal affection for one another, buried the hatchet and renewed their warm friendship in a series of remarkable letters. Adams initiated the correspondence that would last more than a dozen years by writing to Jefferson that "you and I ought not to die before we have explained ourselves to each other."

Gerald Ford and Jimmy Carter

More recently, Gerald Ford and Jimmy Carter waged a bitter 1976 presidential campaign full of personal defamation. Ford attacked his challenger as "cold and arrogant, even egotistical," while Carter contended that Ford was a "dormant, inactive President."

After they were both out of office they reconciled and forged, in Carter's words, "the most intensely personal [friendship] between any two presidents in history," cooperating in many ventures together.

A Call for Civility

★ ★ ★

Almost 172 years after George Washington took the very first presidential oath of office on April 30, 1789, John F. Kennedy declared in his famous inaugural address that "civility is not a sign of weakness." It's a sentiment to which Washington would have enthusiastically subscribed, and with which Donald Trump would vehemently disagree.

As a teenager, Washington wrote into his copybook 110 quotations he found about civil behavior in society:

- "Speak not when you should hold your peace."

- "Use no reproachful language against anyone, neither curse nor revile."

- "Let your conversation be without malice or envy."

- "Mock not nor jest at anything of importance."

- "Never express anything unbecoming."

Throughout his life he modeled civility – always conscious of how his words, actions, and character would be remembered by future generations. He knew everything he did as president was setting a pattern and establishing precedents that would shape the destiny of the founders' bold experiment in democracy. Perhaps Washington's most important legacy is the civility with which he treated others. He was certainly no saint, but he valued civility.

Not all our presidents have been so circumspect. Even Kennedy, despite his poetic and high calling to civility, allowed himself to lob snarky, and decidedly uncivil, broadsides against other presidents.

Just because our presidents have used shocking language about one another, it should not be viewed as a license for us to engage in similar behavior. Nor should the historical use of insults by past presidents be used to justify hyper-inflated vitriolic attacks so prevalent in our current political environment.

Barack Obama once rightly remarked that "democracy is messy." And while free speech is a necessary part of our messy democracy, we should reject what is becoming the slow normalization of abusive language in the public square.

Our survival as a nation depends on our willingness to listen before we speak, search for broad areas of agreement with those of different political persuasions, and reject the acidic politics of personal demonization.

In our increasingly polarized political environment, we need leaders of character – not mere characters – who will embrace consensus, collaboration, and compromise. But we need more than just leaders to set the tone. It starts with us. In our personal interactions with our co-workers, our families, and our friends, we should strive to model civil behavior. Sadly, the comment sections of online news articles and op-eds are often filled with vicious and hate-filled poison. And, unfortunately some marriages and family reunions have become increasingly tense battlegrounds where politics has torn apart and shredded once loving relationships.

In George H.W. Bush's inaugural address in 1989, he issued a call for a "kinder, gentler nation." Perhaps in a "kinder, gentler nation" we could agree on high-level values and ideals while having vigorous yet civil debates over the best policies to accomplish our objectives. We could agree not to demonize the humanity or patriotism of others, but instead to affirm the dignity of others while keeping the conversation focused on the issues. While there will always be differences of political opinion, it is imperative we learn how to treat others with respect and nurture the importance of relationships.

I'm reminded from the preamble to the Constitution that one of the objectives of our great American experiment in democracy is to create "a more perfect union." As we look to the next presidential campaign and election, what might we personally do to help shape "a more perfect union"? What should we expect presidential candidates to do in creating "a more perfect union"? Beyond the policy positions of candidates, are they individuals of character who treat people with respect and dignity and refuse to engage in the politics of personal destruction?

While the policies and opinions of presidential candidates (and the president) are certainly important, their core character and ability to model and encourage civil conversations is even more critical in leading us forward as united states of a great nation.

Conclusion

The caustic and colorful comments of our presidents about one another serve as a first-class dictionary of insults for all occasions. These shocking and funny insults from our very human presidents have been around for a long time. Their very un-presidential words ooze with contempt, ridicule, and hostility. Acting more like members of a college fraternity than members of America's most exclusive political fraternity, their jabbing barbs give us an unvarnished glimpse into their *real* feelings about one another.

As you read the presidential insults in this book, some will ring true with your understanding of the presidents, while you may dismiss others as the product of the political heat of the moment. Some will make you laugh out loud – or perhaps wince. You may be upset by some of the earthy language used. Some of the smears may seem unfair characterizations of a president.

Regardless, the quotations that follow certainly demonstrate the great variety and creativity of presidential denunciations of one another, and their insults and barbs provide a unique insight into the minds and hearts of the men who have led America for more than 230 years.

Despite the negative language often used by presidents about one another, it is my hope this small collection of presidential insults can be used to understand our often-sordid history – but not to replicate it. Rather, may we be encouraged by Abraham Lincoln's appeal that we rise to act and speak consistent with the "better angels of our nature."

May we collectively strive to value relationships over political dogma, encourage deep reconciliation out of our fractured friendships, and reset our political discourse from one of rancor to respect.

101
PRESIDENTIAL
INSULTS

GEORGE WASHINGTON – 1ˢᵗ President

That Washington was
not a Scholar is certain.
That he was too

ILLITERATE,

UNLEARNED,

UNREAD

for his Station and reputation
is equally past dispute.

John Adams (former president) about
George Washington (deceased) [1]
Letter to Benjamin Rush (a signer of the Declaration of Independence)
April 22, 1812

GEORGE WASHINGTON – 1st President

His <u>MIND</u> was great and powerful,
**without being of the
very first order**...

No <u>JUDGMENT</u> was ever sounder. It was
slow in operation, being little
aided by invention or imagination...

His <u>TEMPER</u> was **naturally irritable**...
he was most **tremendous in his wrath**.

Thomas Jefferson (former president) about
George Washington (deceased)[2]
Letter to Walter Jones (former Congressman)
January 2, 1814

JOHN ADAMS – 2nd President

DISTRUSTFUL,
OBSTINATE,
EXCESSIVELY VAIN,
and takes no counsel from anyone.

Thomas Jefferson (vice president) about
John Adams (president)[3]
Letter (in French) from Philippe André Joseph de Létombe
(French consul-general) to Charles-François Delacroix
(French foreign minister) recounting Jefferson's
comments in their conversation
June 7, 1797

The

RASH

measures of our

HOT-HEATED

Executive.

James Madison (former congressman) about
John Adams (president)[4]
Letter to Thomas Jefferson (vice president)
February 18, 1798

THOMAS JEFFERSON – 3rd President

A mind, **SOURED**, yet seeking for popularity, and eaten to a honeycomb with ambition, yet **WEAK, CONFUSED, UNINFORMED**, and **IGNORANT**.

John Adams (president) about
Thomas Jefferson (vice president)[5]
Letter to Uriah Forrest (former congressman)
June 20, 1797

Perhaps the **MOST INCAPABLE EXECUTIVE** that ever filled the presidential chair ... It would be **DIFFICULT TO IMAGINE A MAN LESS FIT TO GUIDE THE STATE** with honor and safety through the stormy times that marked the opening of the present century.

Theodore Roosevelt (New York state assemblyman) about
Thomas Jefferson (deceased)[6]
In Roosevelt's book "The Naval War of 1812"
1882

JAMES MADISON – 4th President

He could **NEVER** in his life
STAND UP against
strenuous opposition.

Thomas Jefferson (former president) about
James Madison (former president)[7]
Spoken on his deathbed to
Thomas Jefferson Randolph (his grandson)
July 1826

He was a

VERY WEAK PRESIDENT ...
he just
COULDN'T SEEM
TO MAKE UP HIS MIND
about anything.

Harry Truman (former president) about
James Madison (deceased)[8]
Oral history interview by Merle Miller in 1961

JAMES MONROE – 5ᵗʰ President

There is abundant evidence of his being a

MERE TOOL

in the hands

OF THE FRENCH

government.

George Washington (former president) about
James Monroe (former U.S. minister to France)[9]
Washington's hand-written notes in margin of book by Monroe,
in which Monroe defends his work in France
March 1798

JOHN QUINCY ADAMS – 6th President

It is said he is a
DISGUSTING MAN
to do business.
COARSE, DIRTY AND CLOWNISH
in his address and stiff and abstracted in his opinions, which are drawn from books exclusively.

William Henry Harrison (congressman) about
John Quincy Adams (U.S. minister to the United Kingdom)[10]
Letter to James Findlay (Ohio politician)
January 24, 1817

His disposition is as
PERVERSE and MULISH
as that of his father.

James Buchanan (congressman) about
John Quincy Adams (secretary of state)[11]
Letter to Hugh Hamilton (editor of Harrisburg Chronicle)
March 22, 1822

ANDREW JACKSON – 7th President

I FEEL MUCH ALARMED

at the prospect of seeing General Jackson President. He is

ONE OF THE MOST UNFIT MEN

I know of for such a place. He has had

VERY LITTLE RESPECT

for laws and constitutions.

Thomas Jefferson (former president) about
Andrew Jackson (Tennessee senator)[12]
Conversation at Monticello with Daniel Webster (congressman). Jackson led in popular and electoral (not a majority) votes but lost when House of Reps. chose John Quincy Adams. Jackson won the presidency in 1828 election.
December 1824

A BARBARIAN

who could not write a sentence of grammar and

HARDLY COULD SPELL HIS OWN NAME.

John Quincy Adams (former president) about
Andrew Jackson (president)[13]
Diary entry on concerns he expressed in a conversation with Harvard president Josiah Quincy on Harvard's plan to award President Jackson with an honorary doctorate degree
June 18, 1833

MARTIN VAN BUREN – 8th President

His principles are all
SUBORDINATE
to his ambitions.

John Quincy Adams (former president) about
Martin Van Buren (secretary of state)[14]
Just one month after Adams' term ended, Van Buren, the new secretary of state,
visited and talked with the former president in the morning
Diary entry from April 4, 1829

Mr. Van Buren's course is
SELFISH, UNPATRIOTIC,
and
WHOLLY INEXCUSABLE.

James Polk (president) about
Martin Van Buren (former president)[15]
Diary entry two days after Van Buren was nominated
by the Free Soil Party for president
June 24, 1848

WILLIAM H. HARRISON – 9th President

ACTIVE BUT SHALLOW MIND ... VAIN AND INDISCREET.

John Quincy Adams (president) about
William Henry Harrison (Ohio senator)[16]
Adams met with Joseph Vance (Ohio congressman) who recommended
that Harrison be appointed the U.S. minister to Columbia.
Adams appointed Harrison to the position.
Diary entry from May 6, 1828

IMBECILE CHIEF

Andrew Jackson (former president) about
William Henry Harrison (president)[17]
Letter to E.F. Purdy (Jackson admirer)
Less than 2 weeks into Harrison's one-month presidency
March 16, 1841

JOHN TYLER – 10th President

Tyler is a
POLITICAL SECTARIAN
of the slave-driving, Virginian, Jeffersonian school, principled against all improvement, with all the interests and passions and vices of slavery rooted in his moral and political constitution –
WITH TALENTS
NOT ABOVE MEDIOCRITY,
and a spirit incapable of expansion to the dimensions of the station upon which he has been cast by the hand of Providence.

John Quincy Adams *(congressman & former president) about*
John Tyler *(president)*[18]
On Tyler's first day as president after the death of William Henry Harrison
Diary entry from April 4, 1841

Tyler has been called a
MEDIOCRE MAN,
but this is unwarranted flattery.
He was a politician of

MONUMENTAL LITTLENESS.

Theodore Roosevelt *(New York governor) about*
John Tyler *(deceased)*[19]
In Roosevelt's book "Life of Thomas Hart Benton"
1886

JAMES K. POLK – 11ᵗʰ President

He has **NO** wit, **NOT** literature, **NO** point of argument, **NO** gracefulness of delivery, **NO** elegance of language, **NO** philosophy, **NO** pathos, **NO** felicitous impromptus - **NOTHING** that can constitute an orator, but confidence, fluency and labor.

John Quincy Adams (congressman & former president) about
***James Polk** (congressman)*[20]
After listening to Polk speak for nearly three hours on the House floor.
Diary entry from January 2, 1834

He is a
bewildered, confounded,
and
miserably perplexed man.

Abraham Lincoln (congressman) about
***James Polk** (president)*[21]
Speech in the U.S. House of Representatives criticizing
the president's conduct of the Mexican War
January 12, 1848

ZACHARY TAYLOR – 12ᵗʰ President

HE IS EVIDENTLY A WEAK MAN

and has been made giddy with the idea of the Presidency …
I am now satisfied that he is a

NARROW MINDED,
BIGOTED PARTISAN,

without resources and

WHOLLY UNQUALIFIED

for the command he holds.

James Polk (president) about
Zachary Taylor (major general)[22]
*Criticism of General Taylor's conduct of the Mexican War
Diary entry from November 21, 1846*

Zachary Taylor

KNEW NOTHING ABOUT POLITICS

and had no set approach to governmental affairs.

Harry Truman (former president) about
Zachary Taylor (deceased)[23]
*Criticism of Taylor's election as president based on his record as a soldier
Truman's Memoirs from 1956*

MILLARD FILLMORE – 13th President

Mr. Fillmore was … a man

MORE AMENABLE TO THE CONTROL OF THE LEADERS OF CONGRESS AND OF HIS PARTY

than the sturdy soldier had been whom he succeeded.

Woodrow Wilson (Princeton University professor) about
Millard Fillmore (deceased)[24]
In Wilson's book "A History of The American People"
1901

He started

TOADYING TO THE RICH,

which he continued to do all the rest of his life, including when he was president. As a result, he was

NEVER ANY KIND OF LEADER.
HE DID JUST WHAT HE WAS TOLD,

and what he was told was not to do anything to offend anybody. Which, of course, meant that he ended up by offending everybody. But

HE WAS JUST A NO-GOOD …

as a president he was … well, I'll tell you, at a time when we needed a strong man, what we got was

A MAN THAT SWAYED WITH THE SLIGHTEST BREEZE.

Harry Truman (former president) about
Millard Fillmore (deceased)[25]
Oral history interview by Merle Miller in 1961

FRANKLIN PIERCE – 14th President

A SMALL POLITICIAN, OF LOW CAPACITY

and mean surroundings, proud to act as the servile tool of men worse than himself but also stronger and abler. He was ever ready to do any work the slavery leaders set him.

Theodore Roosevelt (former NY assemblyman) about
***Franklin Pierce** (deceased)[26]*
In Roosevelt's book "Life of Thomas Hart Benton"
1886

A complete fizzle ...
Pierce didn't know what was going on, and even if he had, he wouldn't of known what to do about it.

Harry Truman (former president) about
***Franklin Pierce** (deceased)[27]*
Oral history interview by Merle Miller in 1961

JAMES BUCHANAN – 15th President

[Russia] was as far as I could send him
OUT OF MY SIGHT,
and where he could do the least harm.
I would have sent him to the North Pole if we had kept a minister there.

Andrew Jackson (former president) about
James Buchanan (secretary of state nominee)[28]
To President-elect Polk,
on Jackson's earlier appointment of Buchanan as minister to Russia
Early 1845

MR. BUCHANAN ...
IS IN SMALL MATTERS
WITHOUT JUDGMENT
AND SOMETIMES ACTS LIKE AN
OLD MAID.

James Polk (president) about
James Buchanan (secretary of state)[29]
Buchanan disagreed with Polk's request to his cabinet that they should not
contact President-elect Taylor until after Taylor and Polk had met.
Diary entry from February 27, 1849

ABRAHAM LINCOLN – 16th President

[Lincoln ruled by]
MILITARY DESPOTISM.

Millard Fillmore *(former president) about*
Abraham Lincoln *(president)*[30]
Letter to John Bell Robinson (pro-slavery writer)
criticizing Lincoln's conduct of the Civil War
August 12, 1864

[LINCOLN]
is to the extent of his

LIMITED ABILITY AND NARROW INTELLIGENCE

their [the abolitionists'] willing instrument for all the woe
which has thus far been brought upon the country.

Franklin Pierce *(former president) about*
Abraham Lincoln *(president)*[31]
Letter to John Hatch George (NH lawyer and political leader) in
response to Lincoln's Emancipation Proclamation issued the previous day
January 2, 1863

ANDREW JOHNSON – 17th President

He is very
VINDICTIVE AND PERVERSE IN HIS TEMPER AND CONDUCT.

James Polk (president) about
Andrew Johnson (congressman)[32]
Observation on having seen Johnson in the crowd at the Executive Mansion
for the president's New Year Day reception for visitors and dignitaries
Diary entry from January 1, 1849

I WOULD IMPEACH HIM IF FOR NOTHING ELSE
THAN BECAUSE HE IS SUCH AN
INFERNAL LIAR.

Ulysses Grant (general) about
Andrew Johnson (president)[33]
Conversation with Senator John B. Henderson (R-MO)
during Johnson's impeachment proceedings.
Henderson voted against impeachment
May 1868

ULYSSES S. GRANT – 18th President

[Grant's]
imperturbability is amazing. I am in
doubt whether to call it
GREATNESS or STUPIDITY.

James Garfield (congressman) about
Ulysses Grant (president)[34]
After meeting with Grant in the Executive Mansion. The president described to
Garfield his encounter the previous day with William Belknap,
his disgraced secretary of war, who had resigned that day.
Garfield questioned the president whether the artist painting Grant's portrait on
March 2 saw any unusual agitation in his face. "I think not," Grant replied.
Diary entry from March 3, 1876

Great gifts combined singularly with a
GREAT MEDIOCRITY.

Woodrow Wilson (Princeton University professor) about
Ulysses Grant (deceased)[35]
In Wilson's book "A Calendar of Great Americans"
1896

RUTHERFORD B. HAYES – 19th President

Mr. Hayes had as
LITTLE POLITICAL AUTHORITY
as Mr. Johnson had...he had
NO REAL HOLD UPON THE COUNTRY.

Woodrow Wilson (Princeton University professor) about
Rutherford Hayes (deceased)[36]
In Wilson's book "A History of the American People"
1901

JAMES A. GARFIELD – 20th President

Garfield has shown that he is not possessed of the

BACKBONE OF AN ANGLEWORM.

Ulysses Grant (former president) about
James Garfield (president)[37]
Letter to Adam Badeau (general)
May 7, 1881

HE WAS **NOT** EXECUTIVE IN HIS TALENTS – **NOT** ORIGINAL, **NOT** FIRM, **NOT** A MORAL FORCE. HE LEANED ON OTHERS – COULD **NOT** FACE A FROWNING WORLD; HIS HABITS SUFFERED FROM WASHINGTON LIFE. HIS COURSE AT VARIOUS TIMES WHEN TROUBLE CAME BETRAYED **WEAKNESS**.

Rutherford Hayes (former president) about
James Garfield (deceased)[38]
After having read "The Life and Character of James A. Garfield"
by Burke A. Hinsdale (president of Hiram College - Garfield's alma mater)
Diary entry from February 21, 1883

CHESTER A. ARTHUR – 21st President

Nothing like it ever before in
the Executive Mansion -

LIQUOR, SNOBBERY,
and
WORSE.

Rutherford Hayes (former president) about
Chester Arthur (deceased)[39]
Commenting on the social life in Arthur's Executive Mansion.
Arthur died on November 18, 1886.
Diary entry from October 30, 1888

A non-entity with
SIDE WHISKERS.

Woodrow Wilson (25-year-old Atlanta attorney) about
Chester Arthur (president)[40]
Said in conversation about Arthur's appointment of members of the Tariff
Commission. At Wilson's law office (48 Marietta Street) with Edward Renick
(Wilson's law partner) and Walter Hines Page (reporter for New York World)
September 22, 1882

GROVER CLEVELAND – 22nd/24th President

A BRUTE WITH WOMEN.

Rutherford Hayes (former president) about
Grover Cleveland (president)[41]
Conversation with his good friend Thomas Donaldson
September 18, 1887

I think
HE IS NOT A MAN WHO SHOULD BE PUT IN THAT OFFICE
[the presidency],
and there is no lack of reasons for it. His public career, in the first place, and then private reasons as well.

Theodore Roosevelt (New York state assemblyman) about
Grover Cleveland (New York state governor)[42]
Interview by a New York Sun reporter
less than a month before 1884 presidential election that Cleveland won.
October 11, 1884

GROVER CLEVELAND – 22nd/24th President

WHAT IN THE WORLD HAS GROVER CLEVELAND DONE?

Will you tell me? You give it up?

I have been looking for six weeks for a Democrat who could tell me what Cleveland has done for the good of his country and for the benefit of the people, but I have not found him.

William McKinley (congressman) about[43]
Grover Cleveland (president)
Virginia campaign speech after 8 months of Cleveland's presidency
October 29, 1885

Damn the President! He is a cold-blooded, narrow-minded, prejudiced, obstinate, timid old psalm-singing Indianapolis politician.

Theodore Roosevelt *(US civil service commissioner) about*
Benjamin Harrison *(president)[44]*
Attributed to Roosevelt while a civil service commissioner,
probably in a letter
Between May 7, 1889 – May 5, 1895

The

LITTLE RUNT
of a president.

Theodore Roosevelt *(US civil service commissioner) about*
Benjamin Harrison *(president)[45]*
Upon approval by the president "at last" of the Indian Rules
for the Civil Service Commission. Letter to Anna Roosevelt (his sister)
July 2, 1891

WILLIAM MCKINLEY – 25th President

NO MORE BACKBONE THAN
A CHOCOLATE ÉCLAIR.

Theodore Roosevelt (assistant secretary of the Navy) about
William McKinley (president)[46]
Attributed by various sources to Roosevelt on different occasions, including related
to McKinley's tepid response to sinking of the USS Maine in
Havana, Cuba in February 1898.
April 1898

His weakness and vacillation are even more ludicrous than painful.

Theodore Roosevelt (assistant secretary of the Navy) about
William McKinley (president)[47]
On McKinley's conduct of the Spanish-American War
Diary entry for April 16, 1898

About the president,
I think I had better not put down on paper what I should gladly tell you if we were talking together.

Theodore Roosevelt (New York state governor) about
William McKinley (president)[48]
Letter to Bill Sewall (his friend)
April 24, 1900

THEODORE ROOSEVELT – 26th President

ALWAYS GETTING INTO ROWS
WITH EVERYBODY.
I AM AFRAID HE IS TOO
PUGNACIOUS.

William McKinley (president-elect) about
Theodore Roosevelt (commissioner NY City police board)[49]
Said to Maria Storer in Canton, Ohio, who was lobbying McKinley
to appoint Roosevelt as assistant secretary of the Navy
Late November 1896

The man is a

DEMAGOGUE
and a

FLATTERER...
I hate to see a man try to

HONEYFUGGLE
the people

William Howard Taft (president) about
Theodore Roosevelt (ex-president and presidential candidate)[50]
Taft campaign speech in Cambridge, Ohio
while fighting Roosevelt for Republican nomination
May 13, 1912

THEODORE ROOSEVELT – 26th President

A very

ERRATIC COMET

now sweeping across the horizon.

Woodrow Wilson (presidential candidate) about
Theodore Roosevelt (ex-president and presidential candidate)[51]
Wilson campaign speech in Springfield, Illinois at the State Fair Grounds
October 9, 1912

Selfish, intolerant, unstable, violently headstrong, vain, and insatiably ambitious of power ... The most dangerous agitator who has ever threatened the perpetuity of government.

Warren Harding (newspaper publisher) about
Theodore Roosevelt (ex-president and presidential candidate)[52]
Editorial in Harding's Marion (Ohio) Star newspaper
the day before 1912 election (Roosevelt v. Taft v. Wilson)
November 4, 1912

WILLIAM HOWARD TAFT – 27th President

PUZZLEWIT

Theodore Roosevelt (ex-president and candidate) about
***William Howard Taft** (president)*[53]
During campaign swing through Ohio for GOP presidential nomination
May 14, 1912

FATHEAD

Theodore Roosevelt (ex-president and candidate) about
***William Howard Taft** (president)*[54]
Campaign speech during swing through Ohio for GOP presidential nomination
May 14, 1912

...the **FAT OLD MAN** who was President. Roosevelt handpicked him to be his successor in the White House as he was

NO DAMN GOOD AT ALL.

He didn't have the slightest idea of what being President meant. At least that's my opinion ... Taft wasn't even in Washington most of the time, and he didn't have any understanding at all of the office ... During the four years Taft was in the White House the country started going to hell.

Harry Truman (former president) about
***William Howard Taft** (deceased)*[55]
Oral history interview by Merle Miller in 1961

WOODROW WILSON – 28th President

The lily-livered

SKUNK
in the
White House.

Theodore Roosevelt *(former president) about*
Woodrow Wilson *(president)*[56]
*Commenting that Wilson "may not be able to prevent
Germany from kicking us into war." Letter to Kermit Roosevelt (his son)
March 1, 1917*

His elocution is that of a

BYZANTINE LOGOTHETE –
and Byzantine logothetes
were not men of action.

Theodore Roosevelt *(former President) about*
Woodrow Wilson *(President)* [57]
*Written press statement criticizing
Wilson's State of the Union Address to Congress
December 7, 1915*

WOODROW WILSON – 28th President

An

Utterly

SELFISH,

Utterly

TREACHEROUS,

Utterly

INSINCERE HYPOCRITE.

Theodore Roosevelt (former president) about
Woodrow Wilson (president)[58]
Letter to William Allen White (newspaper editor and friend)
May 28, 1917

THAT MULISH ENIGMA,
that mountain of

EGOTISM
and

SELFISHNESS
who lives in the White House.

William Howard Taft (former president) about
Woodrow Wilson (president)[59]
Letter to G. M. Wrong (Canadian clergyman and historian)
expressing Taft's frustration with Wilson's uncompromising attitude on the League
of Nations that was rejected by the U.S. Senate in Nov. 1919
March 3, 1920

WOODROW WILSON – 28th President

He has ...
unmistakable flights of
MENTAL
DISTURBANCE.

Warren Harding (Ohio senator) about
Woodrow Wilson (president)[60]
Letter to Harry Daugherty (Harding's presidential campaign manager). Written two days after Wilson suffered a near fatal stroke in the White House
October 4, 1919

WARREN HARDING – 29th President

He has a

BUNGALOW MIND.

Woodrow Wilson (former president) about
Warren Harding (president)[61]
Wilson's contemptuous remark to an unnamed friend
1921

A FOOL
OF A
PRESIDENT.

Woodrow Wilson (former president) about
Warren Harding (president)[62]
Letter to Cleveland Dodge
(wealthy businessman, financial backer of Wilson, and lifelong friend)
August 15, 1922

CALVIN COOLIDGE – 30th President

A
DIFFIDENT
LITTLE
MAN.

Franklin Roosevelt (assistant secretary of the Navy (about)
Calvin Coolidge (Massachusetts governor)[63]
Observation to a friend about Coolidge
welcoming Wilson back from Versailles Peace Conference
February 24, 1919

HERBERT HOOVER – 31st President

A
DICTATORIAL
AND
AUTOCRATIC
PERSONALITY

*Warren Harding (Ohio senator) about
Herbert Hoover (former U.S. food administrator)[64]
Letter to Francis B. Loomis (former journalist and diplomat) expressing concerns
about Hoover, who was being discussed as presidential candidate
January 13, 1920*

That man
has offered me
unsolicited advice for six years,
ALL OF IT BAD.

*Calvin Coolidge (president) about
Herbert Hoover (secretary of commerce)[65]
Comment in meeting with William Jardine (secretary of agriculture)
who was urging the president to promote a farm bill in a special message to
Congress, noting that it would be politically advantageous
to Hoover, who was seeking the Republican presidential nomination.
May 1928*

FRANKLIN D. ROOSEVELT – 32nd President

A GIBBERING IDIOT.

Herbert Hoover (president) about
Franklin Roosevelt (president-elect)[66]
After transition meeting between the president and president-elect
held in Red Room of the White House on
November 22, 1932

Roosevelt was a superb
MANIPULATOR.

Richard Nixon (former president) about
Franklin Roosevelt (deceased)[67]
Comment to Monica Crowley (his research assistant)
September 26, 1992

FRANKLIN D. ROOSEVELT – 32nd President

He was the
COLDEST MAN
I EVER MET
He didn't give a damn personally
for me or you or anyone else in
the world as far as I could see.

Harry Truman (former president) about
Franklin Roosevelt (deceased)[68]
Comment to Thomas Fleming (author)
at Truman's home in Independence, Missouri
November 1970

HARRY TRUMAN – 33rd President

The man is a
CONGENITAL LIAR.

Dwight Eisenhower (former president) about
Harry Truman (former president)[69]
Comment to William Bragg Ewald, Jr. (his research assistant)
Early 1960s

[Truman Administration]
Is going down in history as a
SCANDAL-A-DAY
ADMINISTRATION.

Richard Nixon (senator and vice-presidential candidate) about
Harry Truman (president)[70]
Campaign kickoff speech in Pomona, California
a day before Nixon's secret political support fund was publicized.
Nixon gave his "Checkers" defense speech on Sept. 23, 1952.
September 17, 1952

DWIGHT EISENHOWER – 34th President

He doesn't know any more about politics than a pig does about Sunday.

Harry Truman (president) about
Dwight Eisenhower (general and presidential candidate)[71]
During campaign speech at McKeesport, Pennsylvania in front of a crowd of 8,000
people on behalf of Adlai Stevenson, who was running against Eisenhower
October 23, 1952

A goddamn
FOOL
in the White House.

Harry Truman (former president) about
Dwight Eisenhower (former president)[72]
Oral history interview with Merle Miller in 1961

DWIGHT EISENHOWER – 34ᵗʰ President

A LYING
SON OF A BITCH.

John Kennedy (president) about
Dwight Eisenhower (former president)[73]
JFK's comment to Larry Newman (Secret Service agent) about Ike's assurance
that the U.S. would not need more people in Vietnam to handle to situation there
1961

Eisenhower was as

COLD AS ICE.

Richard Nixon (former president) about
Dwight Eisenhower (deceased)[74]
Comment to Monica Crowley (his research assistant)
November 22, 1991

JOHN F. KENNEDY – 35th President

A scrawny little fellow with rickets.

Lyndon Johnson (Texas senator) about
John Kennedy (Massachusetts senator)[75]
LBJ to Peter Lisagor (reporter) Mike Marlow (TV producer) on airplane from
Oklahoma City to Washington about his enmity and hostility to JFK
as the two battled for the Democratic presidential nomination
May 22, 1960

A BARE-FACED LIAR

Richard Nixon (vice president and presidential candidate) about
John Kennedy (Mass. senator and presidential candidate)[76]
At campaign event in Syracuse, NY,
accusing Kennedy of telling a "bare-faced lie" about Social Security.
Kennedy interpreted it as Nixon calling him a "bare-faced liar"
November 1, 1960

JOHN F. KENNEDY – 35th President

Here was a

YOUNG WHIPPERSNAPPER, MALARIA-RIDDEN AND YALLAH, SICKLY, SICKLY.

He never said a word of importance in the Senate and

HE NEVER DID A THING.

But somehow...he managed to create the image of himself as a shining intellectual, a youthful leader who would change the face of the country.

Lyndon Johnson (former president) about
John Kennedy (deceased president)[77]
Conversation with Doris Kearns Goodwin (author) as part of her assisting him with his memoirs, about LBJ's disdain for JFK as they both battled for the Democratic presidential nomination Late 1960s – early 1970s

LYNDON B. JOHNSON – 36th President

A SMALL MAN.
He hasn't got the depth of mind nor the breadth of vision to carry great responsibility...Johnson is

SUPERFICIAL AND OPPORTUNISTIC.

Dwight Eisenhower (president) about
Lyndon Johnson (Texas senator and presidential hopeful)[78]
Comment recorded in diary of William E. Robinson (his friend) about
Eisenhower's reaction watching 1960 Democratic Convention
July 1960

LYING, CHEATING,
AND
DISTORTING THE TRUTH.

Jimmy Carter (presidential candidate) about
Lyndon Johnson (deceased)[79]
Comment in Playboy Magazine interview
November 1976

LYNDON B. JOHNSON – 36th President

He was a

CALCULATING BASTARD...

He was a

SCHEMER...

Johnson was a totally

POLITICAL ANIMAL.

Richard Nixon (former president) about
Lyndon Johnson (deceased)[80]
Comment to Monica Crowley (his research assistant)
May 23, 1991

RICHARD M. NIXON – 37th President

Richard Nixon is

A NO-GOOD
LYING BASTARD.

He can

LIE OUT OF BOTH SIDES
OF HIS MOUTH

at the same time, and if he ever caught himself telling the truth, he'd lie just to keep his hand in.

Harry Truman (former president) about
Richard Nixon (former vice president)[81]
Oral history interview by Merle Miller in 1961

A FILTHY,
LYING SON-OF-A-BITCH,
AND A VERY
DANGEROUS MAN.

John Kennedy (senator and presidential candidate) about
Richard Nixon (vice president)[82]
Said privately to Richard Goodwin (his speechwriter) about Nixon in
closing weeks of the 1960 campaign

IN TWO HUNDRED YEARS OF HISTORY, HE'S THE

MOST
DISHONEST
PRESIDENT

WE'VE EVER HAD. I THINK

HE'S DISGRACED
THE PRESIDENCY.

I'M A LONGTIME NIXON-HATER FROM WAY BACK.

Jimmy Carter (Georgia governor) about
Richard Nixon (former president)[83]
Interview by Kandy Stroud (journalist), at the Georgia governor's mansion, during
Betty Ford's visit to Atlanta. The second lady, who stayed with the Carters at the
mansion, was launching an arts program
April 5, 1974

GERALD R. FORD – 38th President

Jerry Ford is so

DUMB

He can't fart and chew gum
at the same time.

Lyndon Johnson (president) about
Gerald Ford (House minority leader)[84]
LBJ's comment expressing his frustration with Ford's criticism
of the president's Vietnam War policies.
Between 1965 and 1968

JIMMY CARTER – 39th President

Carter is one of those types who
TRIES TO BE
MORALLY SUPERIOR
but
DOES SUCH SMALL,
PETTY THINGS
that it becomes almost
HYPOCRITICAL.

Richard Nixon (former president) about
Jimmy Carter (former president)[85]
Comment to Monica Crowley (his research assistant)
April 1, 1992

JIMMY CARTER – 39th President

A SANCTIMONIOUS

HYPOCRITE

Gerald Ford (president) about[86]
Jimmy Carter (presidential candidate)
Said to his aides during 1976 campaign

A LITTLE

SCHMUCK

Ronald Reagan (presidential candidate) about
Jimmy Carter (presidential candidate)[87]
Said on the campaign trail
1980

RONALD REAGAN – 40th President

He was one of the few political leaders I have ever met whose

PUBLIC SPEECHES

revealed more than his

PRIVATE CONVERSATIONS.

Gerald Ford (former president) about
Ronald Reagan (former California governor)[88]
Reagan unsuccessfully challenged Ford for the
1976 Republican presidential nomination
Comment in Ford's 1979 autobiography

AVOIDS RESPONSIBILITY,

successfully, for anything that's unpleasant or unpopular or

disappointing or embarrassing or a failure.

IT'S NEVER HIS FAULT.

It's always the fault of his cabinet members, or Congress,

his predecessor in the White House, or some foreigner.

NEVER HIS FAULT.

Jimmy Carter (former president) about
Ronald Reagan (president)[89]
Interview with Barbara Reynolds (journalist) for USA Today
May 12, 1986

GEORGE H.W. BUSH – 41st President

The

MUSHY

MODERATE

Richard Nixon (former president) about
George H.W. Bush (president)[90]
Comment to Monica Crowley (his research assistant)
March 16, 1991

BILL CLINTON – 42nd President

Clinton is a **PRETTY BOY**
who doesn't quite have it together. He's a
WAFFLER
and an
OPPORTUNIST.

Richard Nixon (former president) about
Bill Clinton (Arkansas governor)[91]
Comment to Monica Crowley (his research assistant)
January 17, 1991

BOZO

George H.W. Bush (president) about
Bill Clinton (Arkansas governor and presidential candidate)[92]
In a campaign speech at Macomb Community College in Warren, Michigan
October 29, 1992

The
WORST ABUSER
of woman [sic] in U.S. political history.

Donald Trump (presidential candidate) about
Bill Clinton (former president)[93]
Tweet by @realDonaldTrump
May 17, 2016

GEORGE W. BUSH – 43rd President

I don't think that George W. Bush
has any particular commitment to
preservation of the principles
of human rights...I have been

DISAPPOINTED IN ALMOST
EVERYTHING HE HAS DONE.

Jimmy Carter (former president) about
George W. Bush (president)[94]
Interview in Plains, Georgia
with Serajul I. Bhuiyan and Richard Hyatt (journalists)
July 24, 2001

A **TERRIBLE PRESIDENT**.

He was a

WARMONGER.

He wanted to exert American influence and take
democracy all throughout the world and wanted to be the
world's policeman and started all these wars.

Donald Trump (president) about
George W. Bush (former president)[95]
Said to Rob Porter (presidential staff secretary)
Between January 20, 2017 and February 7, 2018

BARACK OBAMA – 44th President

OUR VERY
<u>FOOLISH</u>
LEADER

Donald Trump *(private citizen) about*
Barack Obama *(president)*[96]
Tweet by @realDonaldTrump
September 5, 2013

He's the founder of ISIS.
He's the founder of ISIS.
He's the founder.
He founded ISIS.

Donald Trump *(presidential candidate) about*
Barack Obama *(president)*[97]
In speech at Sunrise, Florida campaign rally
August 10, 2016

BARACK OBAMA – 44th President

President Obama has been the

MOST IGNORANT PRESIDENT

in our history. His views of the world as he says don't
jibe and the world is a mess. He has been a

DISASTER AS A PRESIDENT.

He will go down as

ONE OF THE WORST PRESIDENTS

in the history of our country. It is a mess.

Donald Trump (presidential candidate) about
Barack Obama (president)[98]
Spoken at press conference in Florida
July 27, 2016

DONALD TRUMP – 45th President

He doesn't know much.

Bill Clinton (former president) about
Donald Trump (president-elect)[99]
Impromptu conversation with customers at New York bookstore
December 10, 2016

The Republican nominee is
UNFIT TO SERVE AS PRESIDENT...
He's
WOEFULLY UNPREPARED
to do this job.

Barack Obama (president) about
Donald Trump (presidential candidate)[100]
Comments at joint news conference
with Prime Minister Lee Hsien Loong of Singapore
in East Room of the White House
August 2, 2016

DONALD TRUMP – 45th President

He appears to

ONLY CARE ABOUT HIMSELF... DOESN'T DO HIS HOMEWORK, DOESN'T KNOW BASIC FACTS

that you'd need to know.

Barack Obama (president) about
Donald Trump (presidential candidate[101]
Radio interview with Steve Harvey
September 28, 2016

GLOSSARY

Bozo: President George H.W. Bush claimed that Bill Clinton was a "bozo." A bozo describes a fool, a dunce, or a clown.

Bungalow mind: This term was invented by Woodrow Wilson to describe his successor to the White House, Warren Harding. A bungalow is a small one-story house or cottage. Thus, Wilson's dig at Harding is that Harding's mind resembled the type of residence that bungalow describes: small and limited in size. Historian Richard Norton Smith notes that when Wilson was asked what the phrase meant, he said "no upper story." [1]

Byzantine logothete: Logothetes were officials or administrators of Byzantium, which was part of the Roman empire. Theodore Roosevelt accused President Woodrow Wilson of being a "Byzantine logothete" after reading the president's State of the Union Address of December 7, 1915. Roosevelt, who was well read in history, was critical that the president, was all talk and no action. A term of profound contempt as used by Roosevelt, the implication is that Wilson was a mere pencil-pushing bureaucrat.

Basil Gildersleeve, retired professor of Greek at Johns Hopkins University stated in 1915 that the term Byzantine logothete "is derived from a Greek word, logothetes, meaning a scrivener who draws up papers. It is the name of a subordinate who does the work of a secretary and holds purely a minor position. I think Roosevelt raked up this scathing term from some history he had probably read recently. It is by no means a commonly known word." [2]

---

1 Richard Norton Smith, "Woodrow Wilson, The Law of Unintended Consequences" (2007). Features. Paper 23. Retrieved from https://scholarworks.gvsu.edu/cgi/viewcontent.cgi?article=1024&context=features.

2 *The Tacoma Times*, "Slings it at Wilson," December 21, 1915, p. 6. Retrieved from https://washingtondigitalnewspapers.org/?a=d&d=TACOTIM19151221.1.6&srpos=1&e=21-12-1915-21-12-1915--en-20--1--txt-txIN-logothete------

Diffident: Someone who acts hesitantly because of a lack of self-confidence. Franklin Roosevelt called Calvin Coolidge a "diffident little man."

Honeyfuggler: President William Howard Taft accused Theodore Roosevelt, his predecessor, former friend, and challenger for the 1912 Republican presidential nomination, of being a honeyfuggler. Specifically, he said, "I hate to see a man try to honeyfuggle the people." According to Warren Harding biographer Frances Russell, honeyfuggler is "a forgotten, but then fairly common Midwestern term meaning mealy-mouthed wheedler."[3] A wheedler is a person who influences and persuades through smooth and flattering words.

Imbecile: An idiot. A dumb, dim-witted, or stupid person. Used by Andrew Jackson in describing William Henry Harrison.

Lily-livered skunk: Lashing out against President Wilson's response to world events prior to U.S. entry into World War I, Theodore Roosevelt verbally assaulted the president as a lily-livered skunk. A lily-livered person is seen as cowardly and weak, while a skunk is an obnoxious or despicable person. Roosevelt's combined vocabulary made his point in a forceful and colorful manner.

Little schmuck: Ronald Reagan labeled his predecessor, Jimmy Carter, in the White House as a "little schmuck," which describes an obnoxious person or a jerk.

Mulish: The phrase "stubborn as a mule" is the source of the word "mulish." Thus, a mulish person is one who is stubborn, unwilling to change, and who does not listen to the advice of others. James Buchanan accused John Quincy Adams of being mulish, and William H. Taft observed that Wilson was a "mulish enigma," a stubborn and baffling personality.

Puzzlewit: Rising from Theodore Roosevelt's exasperation with his successor, he sputtered during the 1912 campaign that William Howard Taft was a puzzlewit. This biting term combines two words that together suggest the bewildered (puzzled) state of Taft's intelligence and mental faculties (wit).

---

3 Francis Russell, *The Shadow of Blooming Grove, Warren G. Harding in His Times* (New York: McGraw-Hill Book Company, 1968), p. 224.

INSULTS IN ALPHABETICAL ORDER

Insult	About	By
Autocratic	Herbert Hoover	Warren Harding
Backbone of an angleworm	James Garfield	Ulysses Grant
Barbarian	Andrew Jackson	John Q. Adams
Bare-faced liar	John F. Kennedy	Richard M. Nixon
Bewildered	James K. Polk	Abraham Lincoln
Bigoted partisan	Zachary Taylor	James K. Polk
Bozo	Bill Clinton	George H.W. Bush
Brute with women	Grover Cleveland	Rutherford Hayes
Bungalow mind	Warren Harding	Woodrow Wilson
Byzantine logothete	Woodrow Wilson	Theodore Roosevelt
Calculating bastard	Lyndon Johnson	Richard Nixon
Clownish	John Q. Adams	William H. Harrison
Coarse	John Q. Adams	William H. Harrison
Cold as Ice	Dwight Eisenhower	Richard M. Nixon
Cold-blooded	Benjamin Harrison	Theodore Roosevelt
Coldest man	Franklin Roosevelt	Harry Truman
Complete fizzle	Franklin Pierce	Harry Truman
Confused	Thomas Jefferson	John Adams
Congenital liar	Harry Truman	Dwight Eisenhower
Dangerous agitator	Theodore Roosevelt	Warren Harding
Demagogue	Theodore Roosevelt	William H. Taft
Dangerous man	Richard Nixon	John F. Kennedy
Dictatorial	Herbert Hoover	Warren Harding
Diffident little man	Calvin Coolidge	Franklin Roosevelt
Dirty	John Q. Adams	William H. Harrison

Mike Purdy

Insult	About	By
Disaster as a president	Barack Obama	Donald Trump
Disgusting man	John Q. Adams	Wm. H. Harrison
Dishonest president	Richard Nixon	Jimmy Carter
Doesn't know much	Donald Trump	Bill Clinton
Dumb	Gerald Ford	Lyndon Johnson
Erratic comet	Theodore Roosevelt	Woodrow Wilson
Fathead	William H. Taft	Theodore Roosevelt
Fat old man	William H. Taft	Harry Truman
Fool	Warren Harding	Woodrow Wilson
Fool	Dwight Eisenhower	Harry Truman
Foolish leader	Barack Obama	Donald Trump
Founded ISIS	Barack Obama	Donald Trump
Gibbering idiot	Franklin Roosevelt	Herbert Hoover
Great mediocrity	Ulysses Grant	Woodrow Wilson
Hot-heated Executive	John Adams	James Madison
Hypocritical	Jimmy Carter	Richard Nixon
Honeyfuggle[r]	Theodore Roosevelt	William H. Taft
Ignorant	Thomas Jefferson	John Adams
Ignorant president	Barack Obama	Donald Trump
Illiterate	George Washington	John Adams
Imbecile chief	William H. Harrison	Andrew Jackson
Incapable	Thomas Jefferson	Theodore Roosevelt
Indiscreet	William H. Harrison	John Q. Adams
Infernal liar	Andrew Johnson	Ulysses Grant
Insatiably ambitious	Theodore Roosevelt	Warren Harding
Insincere hypocrite	Woodrow Wilson	Theodore Roosevelt
Intolerant	Theodore Roosevelt	Warren Harding
Irritable	George Washington	Thomas Jefferson
Lily-livered skunk	Woodrow Wilson	Theodore Roosevelt
Limited ability	Abraham Lincoln	Franklin Pierce
Little runt	Benjamin Harrison	Theodore Roosevelt
Little schmuck	Jimmy Carter	Ronald Reagan

Insult	About	By
Low capacity	Franklin Pierce	Theodore Roosevelt
Lying bastard	Richard Nixon	Harry Truman
Lying son-of-a-bitch	Richard Nixon	John F. Kennedy
Lying son-of-a-bitch	Dwight Eisenhower	John F. Kennedy
Mental disturbance	Woodrow Wilson	Warren Harding
Miserably perplexed man	James K. Polk	Abraham Lincoln
Mulish	John Q. Adams	James Buchanan
Mulish enigma	Woodrow Wilson	William H. Taft
Mushy moderate	George H.W. Bush	Richard Nixon
Narrow intelligence	Abraham Lincoln	Franklin Pierce
Narrow minded	Zachary Taylor	James Polk
Narrow minded	Benjamin Harrison	Theodore Roosevelt
Non-entity with side whiskers	Chester Arthur	Woodrow Wilson
Obstinate	John Adams	Thomas Jefferson
Obstinate	Benjamin Harrison	Theodore Roosevelt
Old maid	James Buchanan	James K. Polk
Opportunist	Bill Clinton	Richard Nixon
Opportunistic	Lyndon Johnson	Dwight Eisenhower
Political sectarian	John Tyler	John Q. Adams
Perverse	John Q. Adams	James Buchanan
Perverse	Andrew Johnson	James Polk
Prejudiced	Benjamin Harrison	Theodore Roosevelt
Pugnacious	Theodore Roosevelt	William McKinley
Puzzlewit	William H. Taft	Theodore Roosevelt
Sanctimonious hypocrite	Jimmy Carter	Gerald Ford
Schemer	Lyndon Johnson	Richard Nixon
Scrawny little fellow	John F. Kennedy	Lyndon B. Johnson
Selfish	Martin Van Buren	James K. Polk
Selfish	Theodore Roosevelt	Warren Harding
Selfish	Woodrow Wilson	Theodore Roosevelt
Shallow mind	William H. Harrison	John Q. Adams
Stupidity	Ulysses Grant	James Garfield

Insult	About	By
Superb manipulator	Franklin Roosevelt	Richard Nixon
Superficial	Lyndon Johnson	Dwight Eisenhower
Terrible president	George W. Bush	Donald Trump
Timid	Benjamin Harrison	Theodore Roosevelt
Treacherous	Woodrow Wilson	Theodore Roosevelt
Unfit	Andrew Jackson	Thomas Jefferson
Unfit	William H. Taft	Theodore Roosevelt
Unfit to serve as president	Donald Trump	Barack Obama
Uninformed	Thomas Jefferson	John Adams
Unlearned	George Washington	John Adams
Unpatriotic	Martin Van Buren	James K. Polk
Unprepared	Donald Trump	Barack Obama
Unread	George Washington	John Adams
Unstable	Theodore Roosevelt	Warren Harding
Vain	John Adams	Thomas Jefferson
Vain	William H. Harrison	John Q. Adams
Vain	Theodore Roosevelt	Warren Harding
Vindictive	Andrew Johnson	James K. Polk
Violently Headstrong	Theodore Roosevelt	Warren Harding
Waffler	Bill Clinton	Richard Nixon
Warmonger	George W. Bush	Donald Trump
Weak	Thomas Jefferson	John Adams
Weak	James Madison	Harry Truman
Weak	Zachary Taylor	James K. Polk
Worst president	Barack Obama	Donald Trump
Young whippersnapper	John F. Kennedy	Lyndon Johnson

SPEAKER/WRITER OF INSULT

Speaker/Writer	About
George Washington	James Monroe
John Adams	George Washington
	Thomas Jefferson
Thomas Jefferson	George Washington
	John Adams
	James Madison
	Andrew Jackson
James Madison	John Adams
John Quincy Adams	Andrew Jackson
	Martin Van Buren
	William Henry Harrison
	John Tyler
	James K. Polk
Andrew Jackson	William Henry Harrison
	James Buchanan
William Henry Harrison	John Quincy Adams
James Polk	Martin Van Buren
	Zachary Taylor
	James Buchanan
	Andrew Johnson
Millard Fillmore	Abraham Lincoln
Franklin Pierce	Abraham Lincoln
James Buchanan	John Quincy Adams
Abraham Lincoln	James K. Polk

Speaker/Writer	About
Ulysses S. Grant	Andrew Johnson
	James A. Garfield
Rutherford B. Hayes	James A. Garfield
	Chester A. Arthur
	Grover Cleveland
James A. Garfield	Ulysses S. Grant
William McKinley	Grover Cleveland
	Theodore Roosevelt
Theodore Roosevelt	Thomas Jefferson
	John Tyler
	Franklin Pierce
	Grover Cleveland
	Benjamin Harrison
	William McKinley
	William Howard Taft
	Woodrow Wilson
William Howard Taft	Theodore Roosevelt
	Woodrow Wilson
Woodrow Wilson	Millard Fillmore
	Ulysses S. Grant
	Rutherford B. Hayes
	Chester A. Arthur
	Theodore Roosevelt
	Warren Harding
Warren Harding	Theodore Roosevelt
	Woodrow Wilson
	Herbert Hoover
Herbert Hoover	Franklin D. Roosevelt
Franklin D. Roosevelt	Calvin Coolidge
Harry Truman	James Madison
	Zachary Taylor
	Millard Fillmore

Speaker/Writer	About
Harry Truman	Franklin Pierce
	William Howard Taft
	Franklin D. Roosevelt
	Dwight Eisenhower
	Richard M. Nixon
Dwight Eisenhower	Harry Truman
	Lyndon B. Johnson
John F. Kennedy	Dwight Eisenhower
	Richard M. Nixon
Lyndon B. Johnson	John F. Kennedy
	Gerald Ford
Richard M. Nixon	Franklin D. Roosevelt
	Harry Truman
	Dwight Eisenhower
	John F. Kennedy
	Lyndon B. Johnson
	Jimmy Carter
	George H.W. Bush
	Bill Clinton
Gerald Ford	Jimmy Carter
	Ronald Reagan
Jimmy Carter	Lyndon B. Johnson
	Richard M. Nixon
	Ronald Reagan
	George W. Bush
Ronald Reagan	Jimmy Carter
George H.W. Bush	Bill Clinton
Bill Clinton	Donald Trump
Barack Obama	Donald Trump
Donald Trump	Bill Clinton
	George W. Bush
	Barack Obama

SOURCE OF INSULTS

Source of Insults	Number of Quotes
Conversations and oral statements	23
Letters	19
Diaries[1]	14
Private	56
Media[2]	13
Oral histories[3]	12
Speeches	12
Books by a president	8
Public	45
Total:	101

[1] Includes book margin notes by Washington about Monroe.

[2] Includes interviews, press conferences, social media posts, editorials, press statements.

[3] Includes oral histories of Truman (Merle Miller) and Nixon (Monica Crowley).

NOTES

1 "From John Adams to Benjamin Rush, 22 April 1812," *Founders Online,* National Archives, last modified June 13, 2018, http://founders.archives. gov/documents/Adams/99-02-02-5777.

2 "Thomas Jefferson to Walter Jones, 2 January 1814," *Founders Online,* National Archives, last modified June 13, 2018, http://founders.archives. gov/documents/Jefferson/03-07-02-0052. [Original source: *The Papers of Thomas Jefferson,* Retirement Series, vol. 7, *28 November 1813 to 30 September 1814,* ed. J. Jefferson Looney. Princeton: Princeton University Press, 2010, pp. 100–104.]

3 Frederick J. Turner, editor, *Correspondence of the French Ministers to the United States, 1791-1797,* Annual Report of the American Historical Association for the Year 1903, Volume II, Seventh Report of Historical Manuscripts Commission, (Washington: Government Printing Office, 1904), p. 1030. Retrieved from https://babel.hathitrust.org/cgi/pt?id=mdp.39015039510204; view=1up;seq=1025.

4 "To Thomas Jefferson from James Madison, [18 or 19 February 1798]," *Founders Online,* National Archives, last modified June 13, 2018, http:// founders.archives.gov/documents/Jefferson/01-30-02-0078.   [Original source: *The Papers of Thomas Jefferson,* vol. 30, *1 January 1798–31 January 1799,* ed. Barbara B. Oberg. Princeton: Princeton University Press, 2003, pp. 116–118.]. While many sources state that this is a reference to "hot-headed" (not "hot-heated"), Madison's handwriting clearly states "hot-heated." View the original image of the letter from the Library of Congress retrieved from https://www.loc.gov/resource/mjm.06_0511_0513/?sp=2.

5 John Adams, *Extract from John Adams to Uriah Forrest,* Thomas Jefferson Monticello: http://tjrs.monticello.org/letter/1753

6 Theodore Roosevelt, *The Naval War of 1812,* Part II (New York: G.P. Putnam's Sons, 1900), pp. 198-199, Retrieved from https://archive.org/details/ thenavalwarof181202roosrich/page/198.

7 Sarah N. Randolph, editor, *The Domestic Life of Thomas Jefferson,* (New

York: Harper & Brothers, Publishers, 1871), p. 427. Retrieved from https://archive.org/details/in.ernet.dli.2015.154164/page/n433.

[8] Merle Miller, *Plain Speaking, An Oral Biography of Harry S. Truman* (New York: Berkley Books, 1973), pp. 343-344.

[9] "Comments on Monroe's *A View of the Conduct of the Executive of the United States*, March 1798," *Founders Online*, National Archives, last modified June 13, 2018, http://founders.archives.gov/documents/Washington/06-02-02-0146. [Original source: *The Papers of George Washington*, Retirement Series, vol. 2, *2 January 1798–15 September 1798*, ed. W. W. Abbot. Charlottesville: University Press of Virginia, 1998, pp. 169–217.]

[10] Freeman Cleaves, *Old Tippecanoe: William Henry Harrison and His Time* (New York: Charles Scribner's Sons, 1939), p. 241.

[11] Philip S. Klein, *President James Buchanan, A Biography*, (University Park, Pennsylvania: The Pennsylvania State University Press, 1962), p. 41. Retrieved from https://archive.org/stream/presidentjamesbu007671mbp/presidentjamesbu007671mbp_djvu.txt.

[12] Fletcher Webster, editor, *The Private Correspondence of Daniel Webster*, Volume 1, (Boston: Little, Brown and Company, 1857), p. 371.

[13] Large image display of John Quincy Adams diary 39, 1 December 1832 – 31 May 1835, page 98. John Quincy Adams Diary: An Electronic Archive. Boston, Mass.: Massachusetts Historical Society, 2018. http://www.masshist.org/jqadiaries.

[14] Charles Francis Adams, editor, *Memoirs of John Quincy Adams,* Vol. VIII (Philadelphia: J.B. Lippincott & Co., 1876), p.129.

[15] Alan Nevins, editor, *Polk: The Diary of a President, 1845-1849* (New York: Capricorn Books, 1968), p. 328.

[16] Charles Francis Adams, editor, *Memoirs of John Quincy Adams, Comprising Portions of His Diary from 1795 to 1848*, Vol. VII (Philadelphia: J.B. Lippincott & Co., 1875), p. 530. https://archive.org/details/memoirsofjohnquiooadams/page/526.

[17] Marquis James, *The Life of Andrew Jackson* (Indianapolis: Bobbs-Merrill, 1937), p. 456.

[18] John Quincy Adams diary 41, 5 December 1836 - 4 January 1837, 29 July 1840 - 31 December 1841, page 298 [electronic edition]. *The Diaries of John Quincy Adams: A Digital Collection.* Boston, Mass.: Massachusetts Historical Society, 2004. http://www.masshist.org/jqadiaries.

[19] Theodore Roosevelt, *Life of Thomas Hart Benton* (Boston: Houghton, Mif-

flin and Company, 1887) p. 239. Retrieved from https://archive.org/details/lifeofthomashart00roos/page/238.

20 Charles Francis Adams, editor, *Memoirs of John Quincy Adams, Comprising Portions of His Diary from 1795 to 1848*, Vol. IX (Philadelphia: J.B. Lippincott & Co., 1876), p. 64. Retrieved from https://archive.org/details/memoirsofjohnqui04lcadam/page/64.

21 The Abraham Lincoln Association, Roy P. Basler, editor, *The Collected Works of Abraham Lincoln*, Vol I (New Brunswick, New Jersey: Rutgers University Press, 1953), pp. 441-441.

22 Milo Milton Quaife, Edited and Annotated by, *The Diary of James K. Polk During His Presidency, 1845 to 1849*, Vol. II (Chicago: A.C. McClurg & Co., 1910), pp. 249-250. Retrieved from https://archive.org/details/diaryofjameskpol02polk/page/248.

23 Harry S. Truman, *Memoirs: Years of Trial and Hope*, Volume Two (Garden City, NY: Doubleday & Company, Inc., 1956), p. 195. Retrieved from https://archive.org/details/yearsoftrialandh000234mbp/page/n211.

24 Woodrow Wilson, *A History of The American People*, Vol. IV (New York: Harper & Brothers Publishers, 1903), p. 140.

25 Merle Miller, *Plain Speaking, An Oral Biography of Harry S. Truman* (New York: Berkley Books, 1973), p. 381.

26 Theodore Roosevelt, *Life of Thomas Hart Benton* (Boston: Houghton, Mifflin and Company, 1887), p. 345. Retrieved from https://archive.org/details/thomashartbento02roosgoog/page/n355.

27 Merle Miller, *Plain Speaking, An Oral Biography of Harry S. Truman* (New York: Berkley Books, 1973), pp. 381-382.

28 Augustus C. Buell, *History of Andrew Jackson, Pioneer, Patriot, Soldier, Politician, President*, Volume II (New York: Charles Scribner's Sons, 1904), p. 404. Retrieved from https://archive.org/stream/historyofandrew00buel/historyofandrew00buel_djvu.txt.

29 Milo Milton Quaife, Edited and Annotated by, *The Diary of James K. Polk During His Presidency, 1845 to 1849*, Vol. IV (Chicago: A.C. McClurg & Co., 1910), p 355. Retrieved from https://archive.org/details/diaryofjameskpolv4polk/page/354.

30 Frank H. Severance, editor, *Millard Fillmore Papers*, Volume Two (Buffalo, New York: Buffalo Historical Society, 1907), p. 432.

31 Roy Franklin Nichols, *Franklin Pierce* (Philadelphia: University of Pennsylvania Press, 1931), p. 521. Original letter at *Franklin Pierce Papers: Se-*

ries 3, *Additional Correspondence, -1869; 1858 July-1869*. 1858. Manuscript/ Mixed Material. Retrieved from the Library of Congress at https://www.loc. gov/resource/mss36194.006_0010_0591/?sp=331.

32 Milo Milton Quaife, Edited and Annotated by, *The Diary of James K. Polk During His Presidency, 1845 to 1849*, Vol. IV (Chicago: A.C. McClurg & Co., 1910), p 265. Retrieved from https://archive.org/details/diaryofjameskpolv4polk/page/264.

33 John B. Henderson. "Emancipation and Impeachment." *The Century Illustrated Monthly Magazine*, Vol. LXXXV, November, 1912 to April, 1913, p. 207. Retrieved from https://bit.ly/2CmLWKe.

34 James A. Garfield, *The Diary of James A. Garfield*, Vol. 3, Harry J. Brown and Frederick D. Williams, editors (East Lansing: Michigan State University Press, 1973), pp. 243-244.

35 Woodrow Wilson, *Mere Literature and Other Essays*, "A Calendar of Great Americans" (Boston: Houghton Mifflin Company, 1896), p. 209.

36 Woodrow Wilson, *A History of the American People*, Vol V, Reunion and Nationalization (New York: Harper & Brothers Publishers, 1908), p. 149. Retrieved from https://archive.org/details/histampeople05wilsrich/page/148.

37 Theodore Clarke Smith, *The Life and Letters of James Abram Garfield*, Vol. II (New Haven: Yale University Press, 1925), p. 1134.

38 Rutherford B. Hayes, *Diary and Letters of Rutherford Birchard Hayes*, Vol. 4, 1881-1893 (OhioHistory.org), p. 110. Retrieved from http://www.ohiomemory.org/cdm/compoundobject/collection/p16007coll67/id/1201.

39 Rutherford B. Hayes, *Diary and Letters of Rutherford Birchard Hayes*, Vol. 4, 1881-1893, (OhioHistory.org), p. 417. Retrieved from http://www.ohiomemory.org/cdm/compoundobject/collection/p16007coll67/id/1201.

40 Ray Stannard Baker, *Woodrow Wilson Life and Letters, Youth – Princeton, 1856 – 1910* (New York: Charles Scribner's Sons, 1946), p. 145. Alden Hatch, *Woodrow Wilson: A Biography for Young People* (New York: Henry Holt and Company, 1947), p. 39.

41 Thomas Donaldson, *The "Memoirs" of Thomas Donaldson*, Watt P. Marchman, editor. Rutherford B. Hayes Presidential Library and Museums at Spiegel Grove. Retrieved from https://www.rbhayes.org/research/the-memoirs-of-thomas-donaldson-1881-1893/

42 Edmund Morris, *The Rise of Theodore Roosevelt* (New York: Coward, McCann & Geoghegan, Inc., 1979), p. 289.

43 William McKinley, *Speeches and Addresses of William McKinley from his Election to Congress to the Present Time,* "What Protection Means to Virginia," A Campaign Speech at the Academy of Music, Petersburg, Virginia (New York: D. Appleton and Company, 1893), p. 192.

44 Edmund Morris, *The Rise of Theodore Roosevelt* (New York: Coward, McCann & Geoghegan, Inc., 1979), p. 426.

45 Theodore Roosevelt, *Letter from Theodore Roosevelt to Anna Roosevelt.* Theodore Roosevelt Collection. MS Am 1834 (325). Harvard College Library. https://www.theodorerooseveltcenter.org/Research/Digital-Library/Record?libID=0281350. Theodore Roosevelt Digital Library. Dickinson State University. For the Indian Rules, see Annual Report of the United States Civil Service Commission, Volume 18, page 233. https://bit.ly/2HCkNc1.

46 Nathan Miller, *Theodore Roosevelt: A Life* (New York: William Morrow and Company, Inc., 1992), p. 267. For a discussion on various sources of the quote see Richard F. Hamilton, *Miseducating Americans: Distortions of Historical Misunderstanding,* (New York: Routledge, 2017).

47 Theodore Roosevelt, *Diary of Theodore Roosevelt from April 16 to August 20, 1898.* Theodore Roosevelt Collection. MS Am 1454.55 (12a). Harvard College Library. https://www.theodorerooseveltcenter.org/Research/Digital-Library/Record?libID=0283221. p. 9. Theodore Roosevelt Digital Library. Dickinson State University.

48 H. W. Brands, *TR: The Last Romantic* (New York: Basic Books, 1997), p. 418.

49 Mrs. Bellamy Storer, "How Theodore Roosevelt Was Appointed Assistant Secretary of the Navy," *Harper's Weekly* (New York), June 1, 1912, p. 9. Retrieved from https://babel.hathitrust.org/cgi/pt?id=mdp.39015033848121;view=1up;seq=616

50 "Teddy's Vanity is Taft's Theme in Tour of Ohio," *The Washington Herald* (Washington, DC, May 14, 1912), p. 1.

51 Special to *The New York Times,* "Clark's Aid Insures Missouri To Wilson," *The New York Times, October 10, 1912, p. 6.*

52 Francis Russell, *The Shadow of Blooming Grove, Warren G. Harding in His Times* (New York: McGraw-Hill Book Company, 1968), p. 235. Notwithstanding Russell's assertion that the editorial was at the end of October, the correct date for the editorial is actually November 4, 1912, and it appeared on page 6 of *The Marion Star.*

53 Special to *The New York Times,* "Victory Surely His, Roosevelt Boasts," *New York Times,* May 16, 1912, p. 1. The date comes from George E. Mow-

ry, *Theodore Roosevelt and the Progressive Movement,* (New York: Hill and Wang, 1960), p. 134, even though his cited source doesn't include the quote.

54 Elting E. Morison, *The Letters of Theodore Roosevelt,* Volume VII (Cambridge, Massachusetts: Harvard University Press, 1954), p. 541n. The date comes from George E. Mowry, *Theodore Roosevelt and the Progressive Movement,* (New York: Hill and Wang, 1960), p. 134, even though his cited source doesn't include the quote.

55 Merle Miller, *Plain Speaking, An Oral Biography of Harry S. Truman* (New York: Berkley Books, 1973), p. 122.

56 H. W. Brands, *TR: The Last Romantic* (New York: Basic Books, 1997), p. 776.

57 Theodore Roosevelt, *Criticism of the President's Message,* December 7, 1915. Almanac of Theodore Roosevelt. Retrieved from http://www.theodore-roosevelt.com/images/research/treditorials/nyt16.pdf

58 Arthur Walworth, *Woodrow Wilson,* Book Two, Third Edition (New York: W.W. Norton & Company, Inc., 1978), p. 104.

59 Henry F. Pringle, *The Life and Times of William Howard Taft: A Biography,* Volume Two (New York: Farrar & Rinehart, Inc., 1939), p. 949.

60 Andrew Sinclair, *The Available Man: The Life Behind the Masks of Warren Gamaliel Harding,* (New York: The Macmillan Company, 1965), p. 115.

61 Anonymous (attributed to Clinton Wallace Gilbert, Washington correspondent of the New York Evening Post), *The Mirrors of Washington,* (New York: G. P. Putnam's Sons, 1921), p. 30. Retrieved from https://archive.org/details/mirrorsofwashing007767mbp/page/n9.

62 Arthur Link, editor, *The Papers of Woodrow Wilson,* Volume 68, April 8, 1922 – February 6, 1924 (Princeton, New Jersey: Princeton University Press, 1993), pp. 112-113. Arthur Walworth, *Woodrow Wilson,* Book Two, Third Edition (New York: W.W. Norton & Company, Inc., 1978), p. 414. According to Walworth, "when a relative asked him what he thought of his successor, he made a noise far up his nose."

63 William Allen White, *A Puritan in Babylon: The Story of Calvin Coolidge* (New York: The Macmillan Company, 1938), p. 144.

64 Andrew Sinclair, *The Available Man: Warren Gamaliel Harding,* (New York: The Macmillan Company, 1965), p. 125.

65 William Allen White, *A Puritan in Babylon: The Story of Calvin Coolidge* (New York: The Macmillan Company, 1938), p. 400.

66 Richard Norton Smith, *An Uncommon Man, The Triumph of Herbert Hoover* (New York: Simon and Schuster, 1984), p. 52.

67 Monica Crowley, *Nixon Off the Record* (New York: Random House, 1996), p. 11.

68 Thomas Fleming, "Eight Days with Harry Truman," *American Heritage*, (July/August 1992), p. 56.

69 William Bragg Ewald, Jr., *Eisenhower, the President, Crucial Days: 1951-1960* (Prentice-Hall, Inc.), p. 32.

70 Richard Nixon, *RN: The Memoirs of Richard Nixon*, (New York: Grosset & Dunlap, 1978), p. 79. Earl Mazo, *Richard Nixon: A Political and Personal Portrait*, (New York: Avon Book Division the Hearst Corporation, 1960), p. 94.

71 Anthony Leviero, Special to *The New York Times*, "Truman Asserts Eisenhower Follows McCarthy Tactics," *The New York Times*, October 24, 1952, p. 16.

72 Merle Miller, *Plain Speaking, An Oral Biography of Harry S. Truman* (New York: Berkley Books, 1973), p. 373.

73 Ralph G. Martin, *A Hero For Our Time: An Intimate Story of the Kennedy Years* (New York: Macmillan Publishing Company, 1983), p. 496. There was at least one other occasion when JFK referred to Eisenhower in a similar manner: "That lying son of a bitch," the president exclaimed in response to Eisenhower not fully disclosing the nature of the Bay of Pigs invasion (p. 324).

74 Monica Crowley, *Nixon Off the Record* (New York: Random House, 1996), p. 51.

75 Peter I. Lisagor, recorded interview by Ronald J. Grele, April 22, 1966, (p. 25), John F. Kennedy Library Oral History Program. Retrieved from https://www.jfklibrary.org/sites/default/files/archives/JFKOH/Lisagor%2C%20Peter%20I/JFKOH-PIL-01/JFKOH-PIL-01-TR.pdf. "Have you ever seen his ankles? They're about so round," LBJ said after his "rickets" comment. According to Lisagor, he then "made a gesture with his fingers" to reflect the small size of his ankles.

76 W. H. Lawrence, Special to The New York Times, "Nixon Says Rival 'Lies' to Voters, Asserts Kennedy Contended That G.O.P. Victory Would End Social Security," *The New York Times*, New York City, NY, November 2, 1960, pp. 1 and 26. John F. Kennedy, *Remarks of Senator John F. Kennedy, Toledo, Ohio, November 4, 1960*, John F. Kennedy Presidential Library and Museum. Retrieved from https://www.jfklibrary.org/archives/other-resources/john-f-kennedy-speeches/toledo-oh-19601104.

77 Doris Kearns Goodwin, *The Fitzgeralds and The Kennedys,* (New York: Simon and Schuster, 1987), p. 780.

78 Stephen E. Ambrose, *Eisenhower: Soldier and President* (New York: Simon & Schuster, 1990), p. 521.

79 Gerald R. Ford, *A Time to Heal: The Autobiography of Gerald R. Ford* (New York: Harper & Row Publishers, 1979), p. 417.

80 Monica Crowley, *Nixon Off the Record* (New York: Random House, 1996), p. 17.

81 Merle Miller, *Plain Speaking, An Oral Biography of Harry S. Truman* (New York: Berkley Books, 1974), p. 179.

82 Richard N. Goodwin, *Remembering America: A Voice from the Sixties* (Boston: Little, Brown and Company: HarperCollins, 1988), p. 105.

83 Kandy Stroud, *How Jimmy Won: The Victory Campaign from Plains to the White House* (New York: William Morrow & Co., 1976), p. 16.

84 Richard Reeves, *A Ford, Not a Lincoln* (New York: Harcourt Brace Jovanovich, 1975), p. 25. According to Reeves, LBJ's aides and history tried to clean up this comment, substituting "walk" for "fart."

85 Monica Crowley, *Nixon Off the Record.* (New York: Random House, 1996), p. 20.

86 Victor Lasky, *Jimmy Carter, The Man & The Myth* (New York: Richard Marek Publishers, 1979), p 300.

87 Douglas Brinkley, *The Unfinished Presidency: Jimmy Carter's Journey Beyond the White House* (New York: Viking, 1998), p. 14.

88 Gerald R. Ford, *A Time to Heal: The Autobiography of Gerald R. Ford* (New York: Harper & Row Publishers, 1979), p. 294.

89 Don Richardson, editor, *Conversations with Carter* (Boulder: Lynne Rienner Publishers, 1998), p. 273.

90 Monica Crowley, *Nixon Off the Record* (New York: Random House, 1996), p. 79.

91 Monica Crowley, *Nixon Off the Record* (New York: Random House, 1996), pp. 60-61.

92 Ann Devroy, "Upbeat Bush Steps Up Rhetoric," *The Washington Post,* October 30, 1992. Bush's attack was actually on both Clinton and his running mate, Al Gore: "My dog Millie knows more about foreign policy than these two bozos." Retrieved from MIT's The Tech online edition: http://tech.mit.

edu/V112/N53/bush.53w.html.

93 @realDonaldTrump (Donald Trump). "Amazing that Crooked Hillary can do a hit ad on me concerning women when her husband was the WORST abuser of woman [sic] in U.S. political history" *Twitter*, 17 May 2016, 4:58 am. https://twitter.com/realdonaldtrump/status/732540713678819328?lang=en.

94 Serajul I. Bhuiyan and Richard Hyatt, "Ex-president Looks Back, Around and Ahead at the Nation and the World," an interview with Jimmy Carter, *Columbus Ledger-Enquirer* (Columbus, Georgia), July 24, 2001.

95 Bob Woodward, *Fear: Trump in the White House* (New York: Simon & Schuster, 2018), p. 314.

96 @realDonaldTrump (Donald Trump). "AGAIN, TO OUR VERY FOOLISH LEADER, DO NOT ATTACK SYRIA - IF YOU DO MANY VERY BAD THINGS WILL HAPPEN & FROM THAT FIGHT THE U.S. GETS NOTHING!" *Twitter*, 5 Sep 2013, 6:20 am. https://twitter.com/realdonaldtrump/status/375609403376144384?lang=en

97 Nick Corasaniti, "Donald Trump Calls Obama 'Founder of ISIS' and Says It Honors Him," *The New York Times*, August 10, 2016. https://www.nytimes.com/2016/08/11/us/politics/trump-rally.html

98 Louis Nelson (Politico, July 27, 2016), "Trump: Obama is 'the most ignorant president' in history." Retrieved from https://www.politico.com/story/2016/07/trump-calls-obama-ignorant-226287.

99 Editorial, (*The Bedford Pound Ridge Record Review*, December 16, 2016), "Mr. President one more question." Retrieved from http://www.record-review.com/record-review/12-16-16_Editorial__Mr._President,_one_more_question.html.

100 Nolan D. McCaskill (*Politico*, August 2, 2016), "President Obama calls Trump 'woefully unprepared' for the presidency." Retrieved from https://www.politico.com/story/2016/08/obama-trump-226564

101 Michael D. Shear (*The New York Times*, September 28, 2016), "President and Michelle Obama Lash Out at Donald Trump." Retrieved from https://www.nytimes.com/2016/09/29/us/politics/obama-trump.html?src=twr&smid=tw-nytimes&smtyp=cur&_r=3.

ABOUT THE AUTHOR

MIKE PURDY is a presidential historian and the founder of PresidentialHistory.com. He writes, speaks, and podcasts on presidential history and politics.

PresidentialHistory.com includes an award-winning blog (PR Newswire for Journalists, Beyond Bylines selected it as their top "Presidential Blogs We Love" in February 2018). In addition to resources about presidential sites, books, and various links, his website includes a popular Presidential History News video series. These short and fun videos recreate and imagine what it would look like if a modern television news anchor reported on key events in presidential history.

Mike has been interviewed by and quoted in a variety of national and international media outlets including CNN, The Wall Street Journal, USA Today, Today.com, Reuters, Bloomberg BNA, The Huffington Post, and BBC. He is a regular opinion contributor to TheHill.com.

He is a member of the Organization of American Historians and the American Historical Association, and participated in the Siena College Research Institute's 2018 U.S. Presidents Study, ranking presidential performance.

Mike has undergraduate and graduate degrees in business (University of Puget Sound), and a Master of Divinity degree (Fuller Theological Seminary).

Sign up for a free email subscription to Mike's Presidential History Blog at PresidentialHistory.com. Follow Mike on Twitter @PresHistory; Instagram @PresidentialHistorian. The author can be reached by email at Mike@PresidentialHistory.com.

MIKE PURDY'S
PRESIDENTIALHISTORY.com